SWAMP THINGS
Animal Life in a Wetland

Wood Duck

by Ellen Lawrence

Consultant:

Bryan P. Piazza, PhD
Director, Freshwater and Marine Science
The Nature Conservancy, Louisiana Chapter
Baton Rouge, Louisiana

BEARPORT
PUBLISHING

New York, New York

Credits

Cover, © Daniel Hebert/Shutterstock; 4, © Alessandro Canova/Dreamstime; 4B, © RC Keller/IstockPhoto; 5, © Alice Cahill/Getty Images; 7, © Linda Freshwaters Arndt/Alamy; 8, © Dean Pennala/Shutterstock; 9, © Frank Vassen; 10T, © Doris Dumrauf/Alamy; 10B, © happystock/Shutterstock; 11, © Millard H. Sharp/Science Photo Library; 12T, © Raffaella Calzoni/Shutterstock; 12B, © edevansuk/IstockPhoto; 13, © Mircea Costina/Alamy; 14, © Paul Reeves Photography/Shutterstock; 15, © S & D & K Maslowski/FLPA; 16, © Derrick Hamrick/Rolfnp/Alamy; 17, © S & D & K Maslowski/FLPA; 18–19, © Stan Tekiela/Nature Smart; 20, © Jaynes Gallery/DanitaDelimont.com/Alamy; 21, © rewindtime/IstockPhoto; 22L, © Paul Reeves Photography/Shutterstock; 22TR, © Stan Tekiela/Nature Smart; 22BR, © Jaynes Gallery/DanitaDelimont.com/Alamy; 23TL, © Denis Vesely/Shutterstock; 23TC, © Birdiegal/Shutterstock; 23TR, © sippakorn/Shutterstock; 23BL, © Holly Kuchera/Shutterstock; 23BC, © Wildnerdpix/Shutterstock; 23BR, © Robin Keefe/Shutterstock.

Publisher: Kenn Goin
Senior Editor: Joyce Tavolacci
Creative Director: Spencer Brinker
Design: Emma Randall
Photo Researcher: Ruby Tuesday Books Ltd

Library of Congress Cataloging-in-Publication Data in process at time of publication (2017)
Library of Congress Control Number: 2016018837
ISBN-13: 978-1-944102-50-0 (library binding)

For more information, write to Bearport Publishing Company, Inc., 45 West 21st Street, Suite 3B, New York, New York 10010. Printed in the United States of America.

10 9 8 7 6 5 4 3 2 1

Contents

Splash Down!

It's spring in the Atchafalaya (uh-chaf-uh-LYE-uh) **Swamp**.

A female wood duck flies between some trees.

Then she lands on the water with a loud splash!

Within seconds, there's another splash as a male duck lands beside her.

Then the pair of ducks swims off to search for food.

Why do you think these birds are called wood ducks?

female wood duck

male wood duck

4

A Wood Duck's World

Wood ducks are water birds that make their homes in North America.

They live in watery places such as streams, rivers, ponds, and lakes.

Their favorite places to live are swamps like the Atchafalaya.

In a swamp, lots of trees and bushes grow from the water-covered land.

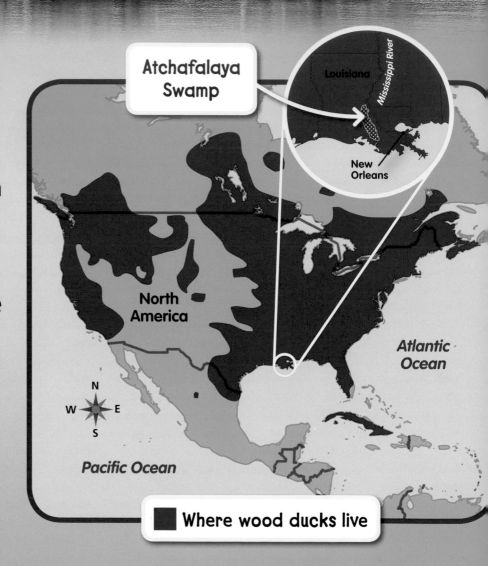

Atchafalaya Swamp

Louisiana

Mississippi River

New Orleans

North America

Atlantic Ocean

Pacific Ocean

N
W E
S

◼ Where wood ducks live

Wood ducks make their nests in trees. That's how they got their name.

a wood duck in a swamp

All About Wood Ducks

Male and female wood ducks look very different from each other.

The male has a shiny green **crest**, a red **bill**, and red eyes.

The female duck is grayish-brown with a white patch around her eyes.

Both males and females have **webbed** feet to help them swim.

They also have strong claws for gripping tree branches.

crest

bill

male wood duck

A Duck's Dinner

A wood duck's main foods are water plants such as duckweed, water lilies, and water primrose.

Sometimes, a duck also eats insects and other tiny animals.

A wood duck finds its food by dabbling.

It dips its bill into the water and feels around for food.

It may even dive underwater to search for a meal!

a wood duck dabbling for food

water lilies

Wood ducks look for food on land, too. They sometimes eat acorns, nuts, and blackberries.

duckweed

Staying Safe

Wood ducks have lots of enemies in their swampy homes.

Snapping turtles, alligators, and foxes all attack and eat the birds.

Sometimes, large owls swoop down from the trees to hunt them, too.

Wood ducks hide from these **predators** in patches of tall water plants.

American alligator

red fox

Wood ducks are most at risk of being hunted when they are babies.

a wood duck family hiding from predators in tall grass

Nest, Then Eggs

In early spring, male and female ducks form pairs and **mate**.

After mating, the hen looks for a tall tree with a hole in it to be her nest.

The tree is often on the edge of a pond, lake, or stream.

Inside the nest hole, she pulls feathers from her chest to make a soft bed.

Then she lays up to 16 eggs in the feathery nest.

a pair of wood ducks

The male duck's feathers get even more colorful during mating season.

nest hole

The entrance hole to a duck's nest is
often very small. Why do you think this is?
(The answer is on page 24.)

Welcome, Ducklings!

After a wood duck hen has laid her eggs, she sits on them to keep them warm.

Every day, she leaves the nest for a short period of time to find food.

After about 30 days, the ducklings hatch.

The baby ducks are covered with soft fluffy feathers called down.

Once the hen begins sitting on her eggs, the drake leaves to live on his own. He doesn't help care for the babies.

eggs

A Big Leap

The morning after the ducklings hatch, they leave the nest.

First, the mother duck flies down to the water and peeps to call the babies.

Then, one by one, the tiny ducklings leap from the nest.

Sometimes, they must jump more than 50 feet (15 m) to reach the water below!

Surprisingly, the tiny babies do not get hurt from the fall.

ducklings peeking out from their nest

Sometimes, a wood duck's nest is not above water. Then the ducklings must leap down to the ground and waddle to the water!

Growing Up

As soon as they are in the water, the ducklings swim around to search for food.

Baby ducks mostly eat worms, crayfish, insects, and tiny fish.

The ducklings stay close to their mother for about six weeks.

Then they are ready to live on their own!

a duckling trying to catch an insect

Science Words

bill (BILL) the beak, or mouthparts, of some birds

crest (KREST) a ridge or tuft of feathers or fur on an animal's head

mate (MAYT) to come together to produce young

predators (PRED-uh-turz) animals that hunt other animals for food

swamp (SWAHMP) a wetland habitat where trees and bushes grow from the water-covered land

webbed (WEBD) having toes connected by skin, which helps an animal swim

Index

Read More

Hall, Margaret. *Ducks and Their Ducklings (Animal Offspring)*. North Mankato, MN: Capstone (2004).

Hipp, Andrew. *The Life Cycle of a Duck (The Life Cycles Library)*. New York: Rosen (2005).

Marston, Hope Irvin. *My Little Book of Wood Ducks*. Apple Valley, MN: Windward Publishing (2003).

Learn More Online

To learn more about wood ducks, visit **www.bearportpublishing.com/SwampThings**

About the Author

Ellen Lawrence lives in the United Kingdom. Her favorite books to write are those about nature and animals. In fact, the first book Ellen bought for herself when she was six years old was the story of a gorilla named Patty Cake that was born in New York's Central Park Zoo.

Answer for Page 15

If a nest has a small entrance hole, it makes it harder for large predators to climb in and harm the eggs or babies.